Day of the Dead

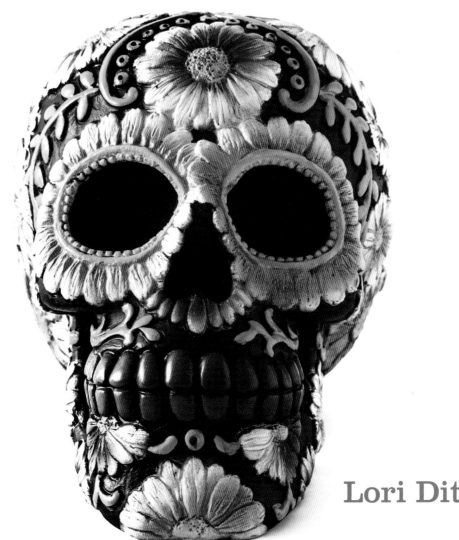

Lori Dittmer

seedlings

CREATIVE EDUCATION • CREATIVE PAPERBACKS

Published by Creative Education and Creative Paperbacks
P.O. Box 227, Mankato, Minnesota 56002
Creative Education and Creative Paperbacks
are imprints of The Creative Company
www.thecreativecompany.us

Design by Ellen Huber; production by Colin O'Dea
Art direction by Rita Marshall
Printed in China

Photographs by Alamy (Lucy Brown [loca4motion], LHB
Photo, robertharding), Getty Images (John Block), iStockphoto
(agcuesta, Amy_Lv, arturogi, BeteMarques, cheekylorns,
ellenkirkpatrick, etorres69, Gogadicta, Oscar Rene Gonzalez
de la Torre, happy_lark, R.M. Nunes, Onfokus, SEASTOCK,
THEPALMER, trenchcoates)

Library of Congress Cataloging-in-Publication Data
Names: Dittmer, Lori, author.
Title: Day of the Dead / Lori Dittmer.
Series: Seedlings.
Includes index.
Summary: A kindergarten-level introduction to the Day of the
Dead, covering the holiday's history, popular traditions, and
such defining symbols as marigolds and skulls.
Identifiers: LCCN 2019053286 / ISBN 978-1-64026-326-0
(hardcover) / ISBN 978-1-62832-858-5 (pbk) / ISBN 978-1-
64000-456-6 (eBook)
Subjects: LCSH: All Souls' Day—Juvenile literature.
Classification: LCC GT4995.A4 D57 2020 / DDC 394.261—dc23

CCSS: RI.K.1, 2, 3, 4, 5, 6, 7;
RI.1.1, 2, 3, 4, 5, 6, 7; RF.K.1, 3; RF.1.1

First Edition HC 9 8 7 6 5 4 3 2 1
First Edition PBK 9 8 7 6 5 4 3 2 1

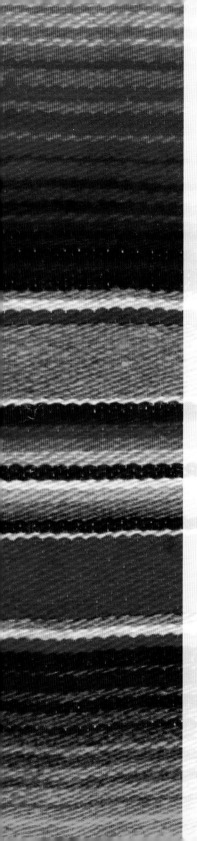

TABLE OF CONTENTS

Hello, Day of the Dead!

This Mexican holiday is on November 1 and 2.

It is a time when families remember loved ones who have died.

Marigolds cover an altar.

Skulls and skeletons show that death is part of life.

Long ago, people believed the dead awoke for a short time. They left food out on tables for the dead to eat.

People in many places celebrate Day of the Dead.

It is a time for families
to gather.

People eat a special sweet roll. This is called *pan de muerto*.

They also enjoy sugar skulls.

Kids and adults dress up. They hold parades.

They celebrate life.

Goodbye, Day of the Dead!

Picture Day of the Dead

pan de muerto

sugar skull

skeletons

marigolds

altar: a type of table used in religious ceremonies

marigolds: plants with yellow or orange flowers used to honor the dead in Mexico

Read More

Grack, Rachel. *Day of the Dead*.
Minneapolis: Bellwether Media, 2017.

Murray, Julie. *Day of the Dead*.
Minneapolis: ABDO Kids, 2018.

Websites

CBC Kids: Day of the Dead and the Sugar Skull
https://www.cbc.ca/kidscbc2/the-feed/day-of-the-dead-and
-the-sugar-skull
Learn about decorations, and make your own skull mask.

National Geographic Kids: Day of the Dead
https://kids.nationalgeographic.com/explore/celebrations
/day-of-the-dead/
Read more about how people celebrate this holiday.

Index